INJURED AT WORK
In California?

Here's Your Guide To Getting
What You Deserve!

Scott M. Blumen, Esq.

Jacobs & Whitehall
73-03 Bell Blvd, #10
Oakland Gardens, NY 11364
www.jacobsandwhitehall.com
Ordering Information:

Quantity sales. Special discounts are available on quantity purchases by corporations, associations, and others. For details, contact the publisher at the address above.

Orders by U.S. trade bookstores and wholesalers. Please contact Jacobs & Whitehall: Tel: (888) 991-2766 or visit www.jacobsandwhitehall.com.

Printed in the United States of America

Published in 2020

ISBN: 978-1-951149-73-4

PREFACE

The once-generous and intentionally liberal California workers' compensation system has been repeatedly gutted by the California legislature in 2004 and again in 2010 under Governors Schwarzenegger and Brown, respectively. As a result, there are now significant limitations on the amount and duration of monetary, medical and job retraining benefits available to California injured workers. Do you remember the T-shirt that said, "I'm With Stupid", with two arrows pointing at each other? That pretty much summarizes what attorneys, claims professionals and clients must deal with on many cases, largely due to the reliance on overly-complicated and technical rules that some professionals believe have caused more delays and denials, instead of streamlining the process.

The only way that there will be significant change again is through the legislative process. Unfortunately, injured workers are not considered a legislative priority, and the statistics about how well this system operates (or doesn't) are always subject to debate.

The purpose of this book is to give the reader an inside view into the nuts and bolts of a workers' compensation claim. It is not meant to be an exhaustive or complete analysis or even a "how-to" book. Life is very short to begin with, and many clients would be much happier, and their cases would go much smoother if they spoke with and even hired an attorney early on in the process. Attorneys can sometimes prevent dire mistakes from happening, instead of trying to fixing the problem once it has happened. Try to think of us as no different from a doctor, mechanic, chef, or computer repair person as you read through this book. An ounce of prevention is definitely worth a pound of cure in many instances. We also know where the land mines and dead bodies are buried.

Dedication

I would like to dedicate this book to my mom and dad, who loved me, supported me, and believed in me long before I ever believed in myself. I would also like to thank my wife and children for their love and patience, and for always listening to me, no matter how many times I repeated the same story over and over again.

This book is also dedicated to all those who wish to reach out for my guidance, as you are all truly gifts from God.

Disclaimer

This publication is intended to be used for educational purposes only. No legal advice is being given, and no attorney-client relationship is intended to be created by reading this material. The author assumes no liability for any errors or omissions or for how this book or its contents are used or interpreted, or for any consequences resulting directly or indirectly from the use of this book. For legal or any other advice, please consult an experienced attorney or the appropriate expert, who is aware of the specific facts of your case and is knowledgeable in the law in your jurisdiction.

The Law Office of Scott M. Blumen
2635 Camino del Rio South
Suite 104
San Diego, CA 92108
(619) 293-4694
www.scottblumenlaw.com

TESTIMONIALS

"From the beginning he was straight forward with me and let me know all possible options. This more than anything is what I appreciated."

– Marcos, San Diego

****

"Let me be clear: hiring Scott and his team to take my case turned out to be one of the best decisions I've made in my life."

– Chris, San Diego

****

"Scott truly cares for his clients and their best interest."

– Nadia, San Diego

****

"Scott took my worries away and allowed me to focus on the more important things like getting better."

– Marcos, Chula Vista

****

Table Of Contents

About The Author

I was admitted to the practice of law by the California State Bar in 1989. I am a certified legal specialist in workers' compensation law. I am also an Arbitrator for the San Diego County Bar Association, where I decide fee disputes between lawyers and their clients. I have served as a volunteer judge for the San Diego Superior Court, hearing small claims cases. I have previously served as a volunteer judge for the Workers' Compensation Appeals Board. In addition, I am a mediator for the United Food and Commercial Workers Labor Union. In the past, I was President of the San Diego

Chapter of the California Applicants' Attorneys Association, which is a lobbying organization supporting the rights of injured workers.

I have given seminars for legal education courses on the subject of physician cross-examinations in workers' compensation cases. Over the course of more than 30 years as an attorney, I know there is a right way and wrong way to do things. I have taken many workers' compensation and some civil personal injury cases to trial. In workers' compensation cases, trials are presented to an administrative law judge only. Civil injury trials are argued before a judge and most often, a jury.

On a daily basis, I put forth my best efforts to protect my clients to the fullest extent of the law. I accomplish this by developing a specific game plan for each and every client. California workers' compensation laws were designed to benefit the injured worker. Unfortunately, this isn't always reflected in reality. Clients are usually confused between pain and suffering, disability, impairment and damages, and which of those concepts even apply in a work injury claim. I will do my best to cover these concepts in this book.

Who Is This Book For? What Do You Want To Explain To Those Who Read This Book?

In my opinion, there are three types of workers' compensation cases. The first type is one that involves an injury that essentially heals up quite well on its own, and results in minimal or zero residual side effects. The injury could be as minor as a paper cut, or as significant as a broken arm; the distinguishing feature is that the person gets all better.

The second type of case is one that involves substantial injuries, and the insurance company is doing everything possible to ensure that medical treatment is moving forward, and all benefits are being paid. I seldom see these types of cases, but when I do, I often recommend that the injured worker, whom we call an "Applicant" (the workers' comp equivalent of a Plaintiff), at least temporarily, proceeds without legal representation. Why try to fix something that is not broken?

On closer examination, is the case really moving along smoothly, with the proper medical professional in charge of obtaining necessary medical treatment? How would anyone who has never been through a claim before knowing this? That said, it never hurts to schedule a consultation with an attorney, and the consultation will be free!

All too often, a case may start out smoothly, but a number of issues will arise along the way. Many clients want peace of mind in knowing that a competent attorney is there to ensure that they are treated fairly and that they walk away with a reasonable settlement. If I think my services are unnecessary, at least for the time being, I will tell the client this, and then advise a check-in after another month or two, until something specific happens. More often than not, either something ***really does*** happen, or the client is tired of "reading the instruction manual" or waiting for a return call from the claims adjuster. Or, the client wants me to take over the handling of the case, just to be able to sleep better at night.

The third type of case is one that doesn't move along quickly, or even at all, for one reason or another. Medical treatment might be delayed or altogether denied, the claims adjuster might be impossible to contact, or the doctors (usually at the industrial medical clinics) may downplay the effects of the injury and send the injured worker back to work with minimal or no work restrictions. This may be fine for a papercut, but it is not fine when the clinic is simply looking to minimize costs and not even bother to see what the injuries really are in the first place! And this practice happens far more often than you might want to think.

Sometimes, clients are offered a ridiculously low settlement—one that would never be approved by a judge.

Personal injury and workers' compensation law are technical and complicated. Both are best navigated with the guidance of an expert. Good lawyers are like computer repairpersons, auto mechanics, or chefs: we know how to fix a problem without looking at the instruction manual each time a problem or new situation arises.

Who Are Your Clients? What Industries Do You Serve?

Our clients are employees; we generally do not represent independent contractors or self-employed individuals because they are ineligible to receive workers' comp benefits. The determination as to whether someone is an employee or independent contractor has changed in California in 2018, due to the *Dynamex* case and Assembly Bill 5, which severely curtailed an employer's ability to classify workers as independent contractors, and not employees. Per the media, these laws affected Uber, Lyft, and food delivery drivers the most, and provoked tremendous controversy. Without getting political, let me just say that employers cannot misclassify a worker as an independent contractor simply by use of the term alone.

Moreover, there are many instances where an employer can attempt to incorrectly or illegally classify a worker as an independent contractor. Therefore, if someone is injured at work and the employer raises the issue of whether someone is an employee or not, it is best to consult with an attorney because this can be a very complicated analysis.

I have represented doctors, lawyers, nurses, construction workers, maids, plumbers, electricians, Walmart greeters, heavy equipment operators, teachers, public safety officers, municipal employees, bus drivers, athletes, celebrities, and religious figures. Once the case is accepted by the insurance company, the criteria for being considered an employee has generally been met and this is not even an issue.

CHAPTER 1

HOW DOES WORKERS' COMPENSATION LAW WORK IN CALIFORNIA?

The California workers' compensation system was enacted in the early 20th Century. The goal of this system was to make it so those seriously injured laborers would not have to sue their employers in civil court for money damages to immediately begin to collect for medical bills, wage loss, and other benefits.

There are several significant differences between the civil tort system and the workers' compensation system. One has to do with the issue of fault. When someone sustains an injury in an auto accident in California, they must prove fault or negligence on behalf of the other party involved in order to collect their damages. In contrast, a fault is irrelevant in the workers' compensation system. If an employee runs a red light and hits a car in an intersection while driving a work vehicle, the employee may also injure herself and the driver of the other car. The employee still has a valid workers' compensation claim, even when they are at fault for causing the accident. They cannot recover in a civil action for personal injuries because they are at fault.

Some people really are a victim of their employer's carelessness or negligence. Their work injury could easily have been avoided if the employer or a co-worker was more careful. This causes tremendous frustration, as nobody wants to be needlessly injured. But, that will not make any difference in the pursuit of a garden variety work injury, unless a penalty is being sought.

It should be noted that 'negligence' is just a fancy term for carelessness or inattention. It is not a crime to be negligent unless drugs or alcohol are also involved. As long as an employee completes the state-mandated workers' compensation DWC 1 claim form and the case is accepted by the employer's insurance company, the employee has a legally recognized claim. However, the severity of the injuries and the permanent effects are usually in dispute.

In accordance with the "exclusive remedy" rule of California workers' compensation (See *California Labor Code section 3600)*, an injured employee cannot sue their employer for a work-related injury-they are limited to a claim for workers' compensation benefits. On the other hand, if someone *other than* the employer negligently (or even intentionally) causes an employee to sustain an injury while at work, the employee can present a civil claim for damages against the at-fault party, through their insurer, and also file a workers' compensation claim against their employer. The term I use for this is a "crossover" case. For example, let's assume an Amazon employee gets bitten by a dog while delivering a package to a private home. She can file a civil lawsuit against the owner of the dog, as well as pursue a claim for workers' compensation benefits from Amazon.

The workers' compensation system has a one percent standard of causation for physical injury. The civil system has a 50.1 percent standard of causation for all components of a claim, including a physical injury. If someone has longstanding, serious back pain and then gets hurt after falling into a trench at work, he can file a claim based on that 'specific injury' (i.e. falling in the trench). If back surgery is recommended, then it may be covered by workers' compensation, ***even if*** there is evidence that back surgery was needed ***before*** falling in the trench. Theoretically, even if 99 percent of the need for surgery was caused by something other than the 'specific injury,' workers' compensation would pay for the surgery.

Most states, including California, also recognize the validity of "Continuous Trauma" or "Cumulative Trauma" (CT) injuries. These claims also have a one percent standard of causation or aggravation. Assume a construction worker notices wrist pain and elbow numbness after 15 years of using a jackhammer every single day. Maybe he doesn't report this as an injury to his supervisor. He may fear he will lose his job. He may hope the problem will get better over time. He may not even think he has a legitimate work-related injury because nothing "specific" caused these symptoms. Months later, the symptoms get so bad, he cannot even hold a coffee mug, or a razor, and the worker goes to a doctor. He tells the doctor about all of this, and hopefully, the doctor understands the law and the 1% causation standard. The construction worker truly has a valid workers' compensation claim.

Unfortunately, many doctors really do not understand this, or do not want to treat workers' compensation patients for a variety of reasons, and sometimes the doctor doesn't advise the patient properly. Worse, sometimes the doctors flat out refuse to treat the patient at all, because the doctor does understand the rules, and the patient is forced to file the claim and get the ball rolling before any treatment at all goes forward in the workers' comp system, and the health insurer may even delay or deny providing any treatment until the issue of causation is decided. Sadly, this scenario arises all too frequently after the claim is reported.

CT claims are common in people who have physical occupations that require repetitive motions. Wrist injuries are common in individuals who use computer keyboards every day, neck and back injuries are common in individuals who spend many years in the construction industry, and shoulder injuries are common in individuals who repeatedly pull heavy mop buckets or perform overhead movements. Secretaries use computers and type a lot, leading to carpal tunnel and elbow tendinitis. In California, the insurance industry would like to get rid of these claims, largely due to the high claims costs across the board. Thankfully, this has not happened, and I hope it never does. We have many honest and hard-working people in our labor force who suffer cumulative trauma injuries. They would otherwise be unable to receive necessary medical and wage loss benefits if these types of injuries were eliminated from the compensation system.

Chapter 2

Are All Employers Required To Carry Workers' Compensation Insurance?

Yes. In California, the failure to carry workers' compensation insurance is a crime that can lead to civil fines, penalties, and lawsuits against the employer.

What Exactly Is A Compensable Injury Under California Workers' Compensation Law?

In order for an injury to be compensable (this means covered, accepted, or recognized) under

California's workers' compensation law, it must meet the one percent causation rule. If the insurance company admits that the worker has sustained an injury, then the claim will be considered compensable and benefits should be provided.

Are Psychological Injuries Covered Under California's Workers' Compensation Law?

Psychological injuries covered by workers' compensation are frequently rooted in physical or sexual harassment, or emotional distress due to being overworked. Psyche injuries are subject to a 50.1 percent standard of work-related causation, not the 1% for physical injuries. Additionally, the employee must have worked for the employer for at least six months prior to the injury. The exception to the six month rule is injuries caused by sudden, violent acts and/or catastrophic injuries. Establishing that something is violent, such as being physically attacked or being held at gunpoint in a bank robbery is relatively easy to prove. Whether something is considered a catastrophic injury, other than amputations, paralysis, loss of sight, for example, is to be decided on a case-by-case basis, according to the California Court of Appeals.

There has been a great deal of litigation in California over whether psychological injuries that result from an original physical injury are covered under workers' compensation law. After the legislative changes, significant limitations have been placed on presenting psychological injury as a secondary consequence of an original physical injury. In other words, if a person was punched in the face at work, they can file claim for both physical and psychological injury. However, if a person sustained an injury to their wrists and later developed difficulty coping with the consequences of the injury (e.g. an unsuccessful surgery, financial fallout from the injury, a divorce, or the inability to return to work), then they would be significantly limited in terms of successfully receiving compensation for the permanent effects of the psychological injury. With that said, it is always best to consult with an experienced legal practitioner for advice on this subject. A person should never assume anything, as there are many subtle nuances within the law of workers' compensation and any other area of the law, for that matter.

CHAPTER 3

WHAT IS CONSIDERED A FRAUDULENT WORKERS' COMPENSATION CLAIM?

Anyone who files a claim for workers' compensation benefits must be 100 percent truthful about any and every aspect of the claim. If someone makes a deliberately false statement, i.e. (one that is known to be false when the statement is made) about any aspect of the case to anyone, severe penalties of up to $10,000 or even imprisonment can occur. There may be civil and criminal penalties for perjury (lying under oath) and insurance fraud. These rules apply to anyone and everyone associated with the claim, including the lawyers, the workers, the doctors, the insurance companies, and the claims administrators. These are very serious matters that are easily avoided when someone is truthful.

Despite what many people may think about lawyers, I will never participate in, condone, or "look away" from any dishonest practices from my clients. If I have any reason to believe that a client has ulterior motives or is being anything less than entirely honest, I will not accept the client's case. We have a zero-tolerance policy in my office, and I am proud to say I have fired fewer than 10 clients over the course of my career due to fraud or suspected fraudulent claims.

With that said, it is important for people to understand what does and does not count as fraud, especially since the news media does such a terrible job of portraying fraud in the newspapers and on TV. It is very difficult to fake an injury, but a person could theoretically injure themselves outside of work, and report it as an unwitnessed work-related injury.

Insurance companies have very sophisticated examiners, investigators, and lawyers who rightfully weed out fraudulent or potentially fraudulent cases and refer them to prosecutors and the California Department of Insurance.

Not too long ago, Southern California experienced a very high incidence of questionable claims. Usually, these claims involved non-English speaking clients that were (sometimes illegally) solicited by lawyers, doctors, and other so-called "administrators", "investigators" and negotiators to present mostly continuous trauma claims to insurers, who would then try to settle the cases for $5,000 or less. Some of the offenders were prosecuted. Although the proportion of fraudulent cases is small, collectively they result in millions of dollars being spent defending and even paying out on questionable claims. When I was the President of the San Diego Chapter of the California Applicants' Attorneys Association, a statewide lobbying group dedicated to protecting the rights of injured workers, I encountered a number of these types of claims. They were easy to spot, and there definitely was a pattern. Short work history, non-English speaking client, claims of injury to the entire body, doctors who I either never heard of, or who had questionable reputations. Then there were the lawyers, and how they used marketers and investigators to drum up business. Many clients were victims, as they never even met their lawyer or had the paperwork explained to them before they signed on. They were signed up by someone at their home or at a fast-food restaurant. Sadly, while there were many questionable claims presented, there were many legitimate ones that existed and were often completely overlooked by the disreputable lawyers.

Some of the dishonest parties made their way into the San Diego market. Potential clients were solicited by leaving flyers and business cards on windshields at shopping malls and advertising on foreign television stations.

I personally introduced about 30 local attorneys who were having legitimate cases taken from their offices by disreputable firms to insurance investigators. These efforts assisted in bringing the fraudsters to justice. Unfortunately, just like immigration and drug smuggling, the prosecutorial efforts have not been completely successful in shutting down all of the attorneys, marketers, doctors, and solicitors, but there were numerous bad actors who were successfully prosecuted and even sent to prison and were heavily fined.

On TV, stories abound of injured workers getting caught on surveillance cameras showing a person water skiing, weightlifting, jogging, bowling, or horseback riding. Is it illegal to do these activities with a work injury? Although that is a question best answered by a doctor, the quick answer is NO, OF COURSE NOT. It may be foolish to do these things, but that is not where the problem arises-the problem arises when the worker denies—either to their doctor, the insurance company, or when testifying under oath at a deposition—the ability to do specific activities that are depicted in a surveillance video. It is therefore absolutely critical for everyone to be honest about every aspect of the case, at all times.

What Happens After I File My Claim?

Once a workers' compensation claim is filed, the insurer or risk administrator has up to 90 days to either accept the claim and then provide medical and wage loss disability benefits, or to delay or deny the claim and conduct an investigation. If the insurer fails to do so within 90 days, the claim can become "presumed accepted", and no new information generally may be used after this time to deny the claim later on.

An employer can elect to delay or deny a claim for no good reason, or even for a malicious reason. For example, if an applicant speaks harshly or rudely to the examiner, then the adjuster might get upset and decide to deny the claim, even if it would seem to be motivated by spite.

If the claim is not accepted but is within the 90 day investigative period, the worker can seek medical treatment up to $10,000. If the claim is flat-out denied, there is a lot of work that will need to be done, and medical treatment and disability benefits will stop. If the claim is denied, there will be the need to obtain a panel qualified medical evaluator (QME) from the state of California to evaluate whether an injury at work occurred. A QME is like a medical referee, and judges usually give great weight to the opinions contained in their reports.

Different rules apply for selecting a QME when a worker is represented by an attorney. If the worker is handling their own claim without an attorney, then the claims administrator will send the proper form to the worker to get the panel process started. The worker will usually have 10 days to fill out the paperwork, select a doctor in the proper medical or chiropractic specialty, and mail it in. The state's medical unit will generate a list of three evaluators, and the worker will select one from that list. The evaluator should generally schedule an appointment within 60 days, perform an evaluation, and send a medical report to the parties.

Here's the rub: which doctor (if any of the three) can capably and thoroughly prepare a meaningful report that would pass muster with a judge if it were reviewed for accuracy, legitimacy, and thoroughness? Which doctor (if any of the three) is fair and reasonable, and understands the applicable laws? Which doctor (if any of the three) drinks insurance company Kool-Aid, and will write a report that's terribly unfavorable to the worker? What if the case is accepted, but the doctor unjustifiably sends the injured party back to work after two weeks, without any work restrictions of other limitations? This frequently happens at industrial clinics. I have often asked the clients if they discussed this with their doctor. Too frequently, the client reports that the doctor sent him or her back to work because the employer pressured the doctor. I know this sounds hard to believe, but the proof is often in the pudding after a new treating doctor or second opinion physician is chosen.

What If The Injured Party Is Off Work But Isn't Receiving Their Disability Checks, Or The Checks Stop Abruptly?

These questions are critical, and common, which is why it's important to consult with and/or hire an attorney during this process. Simply stated, attorneys know which way to move the pieces on the chess board.

I would be willing to bet one dollar that 99% of the workers would never know whether any particular QME, despite their certification, will be honest, accurate, or truthful in preparing a report. Many times, we will tell our potential clients which of the 3 doctors on the list to select, and then advice the client to see the doctor and get the report before retaining us. This is one advantage of NOT having an attorney. If the client is not represented, she can pick any of the 3 doctors on the panel for their evaluation. If the client is represented, the attorney and the insurance company each get to strike one doctor from the panel, leaving the remaining doctor as the default evaluator. I would rather have someone see the best doctor on the panel than be evaluated by the default doctor, just so that I can get a new client.

What Happens When The Claim Is Accepted?

Likely, the worker will be sent to an industrial medical clinic that has a contract with the employer or insurer to treat injured workers. One must ask themselves: do these facilities thoroughly and accurately assess and treat workers' injuries, or do they have a tendency to downplay things in order to keep costs low? That's a pretty loaded question, but what do you think?

Almost 99% of the time, an employer or insurer will have its own medical provider network of doctors, called an MPN. These networks vary greatly in terms of the number of doctors in various medical specialties that an injured worker can see. Unfortunately, due to the amount of paperwork and the low reimbursement rates paid, many specialists have left the system and will not even accept workers' compensation patients any longer. An experienced attorney will narrow down the list of providers in order to ensure that the proper doctor in the proper specialty is chosen. There is more demand for doctors now than ever, and sadly, I do not see a light at the end of the tunnel until there is a major overhaul to our health care system.

All requests for treatment—whether it is for aspirin, an X-ray, or brain surgery—must go through utilization review (UR). The requesting provider must complete a three-page request for authorization (RFA) form. This RFA is based on an algorithm, or formula, and is presented to a UR doctor or nurse who will never even seen the patient! That doctor or nurse will issue an opinion based on the RFA within about 10 days. If the requesting provider fails to substantiate something in the RFA, then it will be denied. This is not something that private doctors generally have to deal with, which is but one reason so many doctors simply refuse to get involved in the workers' compensation system at all.

By the time treatment is authorized, a month or more may have already elapsed, which only slows and further complicates the patient's ability to recover from their injuries. Because of this, treatment tends to move pretty slowly-it's like being pulled over by a police officer every five miles on a long road trip. It could take ten times longer than it would with no stops. Sadly, this situation is quite common, and this is a source of frustration, not only for the injured worker but for everyone else in the system, myself included. Even the claims adjusters, their attorneys, and the judges recognize that UR slows the administration of medical benefits down when it was supposed to be designed to move things along faster! To make matters worse, many private medical providers will even refuse to see a person who is suffering from a work-related injury unless there is an element of immediate danger, harm, or death.

I believe that most of the people involved in this system are relatively well-intentioned, but delays and denials of treatment and increased costs are the byproducts of a system comprised of inflexible rules and busy (often inexperienced) claims examiners who are given very little discretion. As an aside, it is amazing that a system that was designed to move more efficiently and to save money is really doing anything but that.

CHAPTER 4

WHAT IF AN EMPLOYEE HAS A VALID COMPENSATION CLAIM IN CALIFORNIA?

If an employee believes they have a valid workers' compensation claim in California, they should immediately report the claim to their supervisor or the human resources department and request a DWC-1 claim form. The employer is required to provide this form to the employee for any injury that is beyond "first aid". Given the potential for abuse, I tell anyone who has a legitimate claim of injury to request this form, no questions asked.

The employee then must complete the top half, and list all body parts involved in the injury. The employer representative will complete the bottom half of the form, and the employee should be sure to obtain a copy of the completed form. If an employer refuses to complete the DWC 1 form, our office should be contacted immediately at (619)293-4694. We can obtain the proper workers' compensation insurance information from the employer, the California Department of Industrial Relations website, or from one of many other sources unique to our industry.

What Evidence Is Critical In Proving A Workers' Compensation Claim?

Medical reports, witness statements, photos, payroll records, investigative reports, and the employer's first report of injury are all critical pieces of evidence in a workers' compensation claim. If the injury is severe enough, the California Division of Occupational Safety and Health Administration (Cal/OSHA) may conduct an investigation and prepare a report, which may be very helpful in third-party negligence proceedings. Sometimes this can lead to employer penalties. Remember-negligence will not add points to the board in the average claim, but where there is obvious or high risk conduct, a claim for increased compensation for 'serious and willful misconduct' on the part of the employer can be alleged. This is not very easy to prove, as there must be a showing of almost an intent to injure or turning a blind eye to a known serious risk extreme or imminent harm.

Is There Statute Of Limitations To File A Workers' Compensation Claim In The State Of CA?

A statute of limitations is a specific period of time that a party has to initiate legal proceedings. If too much time passes, a party may not be able to receive or recover the benefits she otherwise desires. That's a very general definition! A workers' compensation claim should be reported to the employer within 24 hours of the onset of injury, and certainly not more than 30 days after it happens. The failure to file the claim, at all, within one year after the injury, or two years after the date of receipt of the last medical treatment, may also prevent recovery. Although there are plenty of exceptions, it is never wise to delay reporting a claim to the employer, especially if something distinct happens. Usually, this is not even an issue. Sometimes something distinct happens, like a fall at work, but the employee hopes that the low back pain will subside in a few days. This may or may not happen, so it is advised to report the injury anyway.

In cumulative trauma or repetitive motion cases, the worker and/or the physician are often unaware of exactly how the law applies, or that it even applies at all. Many doctors do not ***even believe*** these claims are legitimate or valid. Many clients have told me they think they only can file a claim for a specific injury. Once a worker is advised by the doctor that the injury ***is*** work-related, ***and*** there is a period of disability (paid or unpaid time off of work, receipt of state or private disability benefits), a two-year statute of limitations generally applies to file the claim. These time frames are usually liberally construed in favor of the injured worker by the administrative law judges.

CHAPTER 5

WHAT IF THE EMPLOYEE IS PARTIALLY AT FAULT?

Again, the workers' compensation system is a no-fault system, which means any fault on behalf of the injured worker is usually (but not always) irrelevant for purposes of an ordinary work injury claim. One exception that is often claimed is in situations where there is a fight between employees. If the claimant "threw the first punch", the claim is often denied on the basis of the injured worked being the 'initial aggressor.' Even if the claimant simply defended himself, this defense is often used as well.

If the injured worker is alleged to have committed 'serious and willful misconduct' (reckless behavior, or working with drugs or alcohol in the system) causing the injury, their claim could be reduced proportionately to a fault, but I have not seen this raised successfully. This is probably because I generally would not want to take a case fitting this parameter.

It is rather common for people who drive (or drive a lot) for work to get involved in vehicle collisions and get hurt, sometimes seriously, whether or not they are at fault. If a UPS driver runs a red light and strikes another vehicle, causing severe injuries to themselves and the other driver, their injury should be covered by workers' compensation. In this scenario, the employer's liability insurance should cover the other party's losses. If the employee were to be sued by the other person, the case would proceed in the superior court that has jurisdiction over the claim.

Does An Injured Worker Have To Be At The Physical Place Of Employment To Qualify For Workers' Compensation?

The short answer is yes. If the employer requires the employee to travel to and from a worksite, then an injury sustained while traveling to and from a worksite or the home office or a client's residence/business should be covered. If an employee gets hurt while traveling out of town for a convention that is company sponsored or required, then the injury should be covered. However, if the out of town travel is optional, not required, or is not primarily for a business purpose benefitting the employer, an injury sustained out of town is not covered.

Generally, an employee is not covered while traveling to or from work, unless they are in a company vehicle. Once the employee arrives in the parking lot, any injury they sustain should be covered. This is commonly referred to as the "going and coming" rule. Injuries that are sustained during meal breaks or during the course of running errands requested by the employer are frequently covered.

What about people who get hurt at the company picnic or softball game? I was successful in obtaining compensation for a worker who sustained a traumatic knee injury in a collision that occurred while playing basketball on a makeshift court located at the worksite. Although the employee was on a paid rest break during a graveyard shift, the court held that the injury was work-related. While this activity is both optional and recreational, there is a "benefit" to the employer in engaging in such activities as a means of releasing stress, and the employer did not require the employee to clock out before playing.

CHAPTER 6

CAN AN INJURED WORKER CHOOSE A DOCTOR TO EVALUATE THEIR WORK-RELATED INJURY?

At the time of hire, some employers will allow new employees to sign a pre-designation form that allows them to choose their doctor in the event that they sustain a work-related injury. I would say that the overwhelming majority of employers in the state of California have a medical provider network (MPN) in place, and an injured worker must see doctors within that network for their work injuries.

If the employer does not have a medical provider network, then the injured worker has free choice and can see whichever doctor is willing to accept a workers' compensation claim. The problem is that fewer and fewer private doctors are willing to work with workers' compensation patients. As a result, finding a doctor who practices within reasonable geographical proximity to where the worker lives or works is becoming increasingly challenging.

Once I have been retained to work on a case, the first thing I do is look at the employer's medical provider network to determine which doctor would be the best choice for the case. Next, I will determine whether that doctor can see my client quickly, and whether they or the staff have the capacity to communicate well in a foreign language. If the injured worker speaks a language other than English, then an interpreter for medical appointments is required and is paid for by the insurance company.

We are in a world where the doctors are being paid less and are required to fill out more and more paperwork, sometimes seemingly for unnecessary reasons. They must see more patients than ever just to break even. As a result, we have fewer specialists such as surgeons, neurologists, internal medicine doctors, and the like, who will see workers' comp patients at all. This has the ripple effect of creating frustrating delays, and wasted time off of work as the two year period for collecting temporary disability benefits continues to run.

Sometimes clients are forced to treat with their insurance doctors, but that is also problematic. Most managed care or low-income medical plans do not allow their doctors to provide medical treatment for their patients within their health plan if the injury is alleged as being work-related. Worse, when a claim is denied, or a body part is disputed, medical treatment in the work comp system is on hold. It is totally unfair for the private health insurer to deny treatment under these circumstances, but I see it happen every day. I have advised my clients under these circumstances to call patient services and explain what is happening. I have seen some success getting treatment if the client is willing to be persistent, but often clients give up or give in and do nothing when they are denied.

What Information Should I Share With My Doctor After A Work-Related Injury?

It is a crime not to disclose prior or subsequent medical conditions and treatment to a physician (or anyone else associated with the claim) who inquires in that regard or to deny the existence of prior relevant conditions when asked. In some cases, a doctor will write in their report that the patient denies any prior injuries, yet we will learn through the discovery process that the person had numerous prior physical injuries—perhaps even an injury to the same part of the body that is the subject of the current claim. Is this due to a lying patient or a boilerplate/recycled medical report from another case?

I have frequently seen inaccurate, incomplete, and poorly written medical reports many times over the course of my career. An injured worker should always tell their physician as much as they can remember about allergic reactions, prior surgeries, prior treatment, claims, and significant medical conditions, for obvious reasons.

Most of the doctors that we refer our clients to for treatment are genuinely sympathetic to them. Nowadays, doctors must advocate more for the patient than for the insurance companies. Therefore, it is absolutely critical that clients are honest and accurate with all of the information they provide to their doctor. Problems arise when injured workers deny having had prior injuries, despite ample evidence to the contrary. Once that evidence surfaces, it will appear as insurance fraud on the part of the client. There is a difference between exaggerating pains and denying prior conditions and treatment. I do recognize that some people simply forget, are poor historians, or there can be a language barrier. For my purposes, it is pretty easy to see which people fit into this category, and which people are blatantly dishonest.

Can My Medical History Be Used Against Me In A Workers' Compensation Claim?

Once a person has an accepted injury and the body parts are ascertained, the one percent rule of causation applies. Therefore, if a person who has an underlying shoulder disorder sustains a new shoulder injury, medical treatment cannot be denied simply because of the underlying medical condition that predated the claim. However, at the time of settlement of the claim, the physician or QME will prepare a "permanent and stationary report." To complete this report, the physician or QME will do an examination and then conduct an anatomical rating of the "permanent impairment" of the particular body part involved, and in doing so, the doctor or QME must take into consideration pre-existing medical conditions. This will be more fully discussed later on in the Chapter.

CHAPTER 7

WHAT CAN CAUSE A WORKERS' COMPENSATION CLAIM TO BE DENIED?

There are many reasons why claims are denied. Frequently, the insurance company cannot complete their investigation within 90 days, and they must then deny the claim, or be forced to provide benefits. Another reason claims are denied is when they are from an unwitnessed accident. Another reason may be that the employee reported the unwitnessed accident right before or after a 3 day weekend, accompanied by a very short time of having worked for the employer. Sometimes, the claim itself just seems "fishy" or questionable. These types of cases just smack of something that is just not kosher. I have seen cases where injuries were alleged by people who never even worked for the employer. I have seen cases filed with an injury date that was before the person was ever hired by the employer, or long after the person was let go from their employment. On that subject, I believe the most common reason for a denial is filing a claim after being fired from their job, as opposed to being laid off or furloughed. In California, the "post-termination" defense refers to situations where an employee never reports an injury as being work-related while employed, but only after they have been terminated by the employer.

An exception to this defense is when the employer has actual knowledge of the injury, or when medical treatment has occurred or been paid for by the employer before the termination. We have seen many cases where an employee notifies their supervisor that they feel they got hurt at work, but the supervisor ignores them, intimidates or threatens to retaliate against them, or even fires them on the spot. Sadly, since San Diego borders Mexico, we still see cases where the employer threatens to have a worker deported if she files a claim for a work injury. Under California Labor Code section 132, it is a misdemeanor for an employer to discriminate in any way (including discharge or threat of discharge), against an employee who has filed or is thinking about filing a workers' compensation claim or an employee who has received a workers' compensation award.

As I wrote earlier, many clients do not understand continuous trauma injuries. We have represented many childcare workers and preschool teachers who have serious neck, back, shoulder, knee, ankle, elbow, or hand pain that is caused or made worse by lifting toddlers every day. Over a period of time, these people develop problems and frequently don't say anything to the employer; if they do, sometimes the employer won't provide them with a claim form. Some employers have a culture at work that looks down on those who file work injury claims. Sometimes employers also do not understand that continuous trauma claims are legally valid in California.

If under these circumstances an employee were to see a doctor who recommends medical treatment, I always get the medical records for my review. More often than not, the doctor never told them their injuries were work-related. If it was never discussed between the doctor and the patient (which is usually the case), then there would be a valid claim for workers' compensation benefits. In other words, as long as the person has no notice of disability from a doctor or knowledge that the injury is work-related, then a claim should proceed.

In the agricultural industry, many workers are hired illegally and without proper documentation. Employers cannot, and must not, be allowed to make intimidating threats (e.g. deportation, prosecution) to employees in order to avoid reports of work-related injuries. This is a crime, but it still happens.

In California, the practice of hiring people to work illegally or with false documentation is widespread. Therefore, these workers ***are, in fact*** eligible to receive workers' compensation medical and disability benefits. On its face, this may not seem right. However, in many cases, the employer is very well-aware they are hiring illegal workers at a very cheap price to perform hard labor. The employers know very well that the employee does not have proper documentation to be hired, yet they are hired anyway. Believe it or not, this is more of an immigration problem than it is a California workers' compensation problem. We have successfully represented many people who work in the state of California illegally, but who have serious work injuries.

Even if a claim is accepted, insurance companies will frequently dispute the severity or permanency of the injuries, or argue about pre-existing medical conditions. Insurance companies often believe that when it comes to workers' compensation claims, both the workers and attorneys play the "body parts game,"- this means that additional injuries that weren't initially reported will be added to the claim after a lawyer gets hired. If the initial injury is to the left knee, an injury to the right knee, low back, and/or a psychological injury is added, just to raise the stakes.

Many of these claims are in fact legitimate, due to overuse or secondary consequences. I have never, and will never, allege a body part or secondary consequence unless I believe it is a just and valid claim. One problem I see quite often is that some doctors just refuse to add the secondary body part because they have been told by the employer representative that they only have the authority to treat the injury that was first reported by the patient. Even worse, some doctors are told by employers or the insurance companies that if they add other body parts later on in the claim at the request of the attorney, their contract with the medical provider network will ultimately be terminated.

While it's very true that many of these claims are legitimate, many aren't. To elaborate, there are many instances of abusive practice where the worker has one or two specific and treated body parts involved before an injury is hired. After the attorney is hired, the first thing the lawyer does is add the entire body system. These are called "skin and contents" cases. Some attorneys use this practice as a business model. For example, they might allege sleep deprivation, psychological injuries, and sexual dysfunction or medication side effects as a consequence of a physical injury, just for the sake of increasing the costs for the insurance company in defending the claim.

I have, and still do handle, many cases that legitimately involve numerous body parts. It is both improper and unethical, and even fraudulent, to knowingly engage in the practice of adding body parts for the sole purpose of increasing litigation costs. Even in cases where the client is leaning on the doctor and attorney to add a body part, it creates a "boy-who-cried-wolf" situation, and these types of attorneys, at a minimum, lose credibility with the insurance companies, the judges and other attorneys. I completely frown on this practice will avoid it at all costs. As an attorney with over 30 years' worth of experience as a lawyer and former private investigator, I understand the importance of conducting a thorough evaluation at the beginning of a case, as this is what allows me to get a sense of whether the client is being honest and straightforward.

Not too long ago, I was accused by a lawyer who represented an unhappy client (translated: He didn't think I got him enough money so he refused the settlement) of not adding a shoulder injury to a longstanding low back injury claim. The client terminated my services and hired an attorney who just happened to be under indictment, after two brushes with the State Bar. The attorney told me that the client was dissatisfied with me because I failed to add the shoulder "injury" to the claim, and that "I never should play doctor" in determining whether a body part should be included or not when the client requests it. Interestingly, there was no mention of a shoulder injury in any of the medical records, and nothing mentioned before the settlement offer was rejected by the client. It was only after the client hired another lawyer that the shoulder was ever mentioned.

I did lose a client and potentially a bigger fee when I was dismissed as the attorney. That did not matter, because there is no amount of money ever worth putting my reputation at risk. While there are some attorneys who obviously don't care about this, fortunately most attorneys I know do care. We always hear stories about the bad apples, but seldom about those who devote their lives to taking care of others who lack the expertise to do this on their own.

That said, the attorneys should give each client the benefit of the doubt when it comes to secondary consequences of an original physical injury. However, I can call nonsense if I see it. If a client tells me that they have been telling the doctor for two years that they have a secondary consequence, but the doctor just won't write it down in the record, then I will try to remedy that problem by obtaining a new treating physician or initiating the QME process. There is an old saying that "If it isn't in the record, it doesn't exist," and that is generally true except in situations where a doctor refuses to notate a body part simply because the insurance company hasn't given them authorization to treat or even examine the body part. A critical distinction must be made here between **notating** a body part and **treating** a body part. A doctor is supposed to document in the medical record all complaints made by the patient, regardless of whether they are authorized to treat or even examine the associated body part. Sometimes, doctors will mention in their report that the patient is complaining of a secondary consequence, but that the insurance company won't authorize them to treat that body part. To me, those notations are worth their weight in gold.

Insurance companies closely scrutinize medical records, claimants, and attorneys. I am proud to say that we have a zero-tolerance policy in our office for fraud. When people have unusual situations, I will do my best to determine whether or not they are legitimate. I am very grateful that most of the clients who consult with me are referred by reputable attorneys, physicians, former clients, and members of my community. Hiring an ethical and honest attorney can make a huge difference in any case. It is no secret that some insurance companies have a reputation of being fairer and more honest than others; the exact same thing can be said about attorneys.

CHAPTER 8

HOW ARE WORKERS' COMPENSATION BENEFITS CALCULATED IN CALIFORNIA?

In California, temporary total disability benefits for 2020 are calculated at two-thirds of average weekly wages, with the minimum benefits rate being $194.91 per week and the maximum rate being $1,299.43 per week. These figures usually are adjusted annually. The first 3 days after an injury are excluded. Payments are made on a specific day every 2 weeks. In most cases, there is a 104 week period of time that an injured worker can receive these disability benefits. There are exceptions for amputations, loss of sight, paralysis and kidney failure, and payments can continue for 5 years.

Basically, if an injured worker is given work restrictions, (no lifting over 10 lbs., no repeated bending and stooping) and their employer cannot accommodate those restrictions, then the worker will be considered temporarily partially disabled, but will be paid as though they are totally disabled.

Problems arise when employers do not provide accurate wage statements for the 52-week period prior to the injury. This often results in the worker being paid their benefits at a lower rate than they are entitled. I have seen employers improperly calculate wages by providing net pay (i.e. pay after taxes and other withdrawals) as opposed to gross pay. Recently, I assisted a client in recovering nearly $17,000 in lump sum benefits. The employer calculated the wages by using net pay instead of gross pay. As a result, the client was paid almost $163 less per week than she should have been receiving for a two year period!

In the construction industry, employer representatives sometimes try to lower the average weekly wage when there are sporadic hours worked during certain weeks of the year. For example, a recently-hired worker might not have any wage information for the prior year, or an employer might pay the employee in cash and keep no records. There are many variations of the same theme; it is our responsibility to look into whether the worker is being paid properly, and the client should never hesitate to inquire whether they are being paid at the proper rate. If it is determined that the rate is not proper, the case can be set for a hearing with a judge, who will determine the proper rate. Sometimes, if error is minor, the difference can be paid at the end of the case when the entire case gets settled.

Why And How Will Insurance Companies Attempt To Use Delay Tactics When Handling A Workers' Compensation Claim?

We have all heard the golden rule that "He who has the gold makes the rules." If an insurance company wants to save money and stall someone into accepting a lower settlement, of if they simply want to deny medical treatment at all costs after the two-year period to collect wage loss disability benefits expires, they can certainly be successful doing that. I cannot imagine an insurer ever admitting to doing this. In large cases involving high impairment ratings, chronic illness and total inability to work, it can take many years for myself and the insurance company to develop meaningful evidence that could lead to large recovery. In my opinion, if you combine these factors with an already overloaded, inefficient system of dispute resolution, sometimes our clients have to ask themselves how long they can hang in there before deciding to accept a settlement. Remember this-settlement only means you know what you are getting and when you are getting it. It does not mean you are getting the most or the least you could ever get if you played out the scenario until the very end. There is also an old saying-"A bad settlement is still better than a good trial". Unfortunately, there is more than a shred of truth to this.

CHAPTER 9

FACTORS TO CONSIDER BEFORE SETTLING YOUR WORKERS' COMPENSATION CASE

Deciding when to accept a settlement offer can be complicated and confusing. Imagine, for example, that a claimant is four years into their workers' compensation case and is now being offered a $50,000 lump sum settlement in exchange for signing a "compromise and release" document, which would mean relinquishing their right to all future benefits. The claimant knows that if they accept the offer, they'll receive the check within 30 days. Sounds like a deal, right? Well, not necessarily. What if the value of the claim is actually $100,000, or even half a million dollars? How would the claimant know what is a fair and reasonable offer, and at what point should they just accept the offer?

Every doctor who evaluates or treats someone for a work-related injury needs to write a report consistent with the 5th Edition of AMA Guides to the Evaluation of Permanent Impairment. (Other states use the 6th Edition.) In that report, the doctor should make a calculation of the percentage of what's called "whole person impairment," which rates the worker's injuries as a proportion of the rest of their body. This calculation is based upon the effects that the injuries have had on the worker's daily life (e.g. cooking, cleaning, dressing, etc.). In theory, every medical evaluator should be able to plug in certain terms and come up with the proper percentages for a given body part or parts. The spine has "scheduled ratings" for 5 different categories. Shoulder, hands, wrists, elbows and knees are mostly based on the range of motion method, but the examiner has leeway to use strength loss. There can be an increase of up to 3% for pain for an orthopedic injury. Pain can be rated separately if there is a specific pain disorder. A complaint of pain in a body part alone generally will not trigger a separate pain rating. Injured workers should not suffer due to their ignorance of the nuances of a highly technical and outdated compensation system that calls an impairment rating a "permanent disability". We know that a disability is an inability to work, but an impairment is an anatomical dysfunction. The two concepts are quite different, but have been blended together by the California legislature. Beyond that, a workers' compensation settlement is based upon an impairment rating, not by how much pain or inability to work exists at the time the patient is released from active medical care.

All settlements for all cases—with or without an attorney—must be presented to a workers' compensation administrative law judge. The papers are to be presented on pre-printed, state-approved OCR bar-coded forms. They must be properly filled out for scanning into the state's paperless system. If a claimant does not have an attorney, then they will have to mail in the completed forms. If the papers are incorrectly filled out (and we still attend day-long seminars to learn how to do this), then they will be rejected, and the judge probably will never see them.

Once the judge receives the forms, they are obligated to thoroughly review the settlement. Since there are far too many considerations for the judge to make a quick decision, the judge will send the case to an information and assistance officer who works for the State Division of Workers' Compensation. This officer should meet with the claimant and review the settlement. Maybe three or six months later, the case will be sent back to the judge and it may be set for a hearing. While the case may really be worth three to four times the offer, the insurance company will refuse to pay that amount, and the judge should not approve the settlement. As a result, the claimant's case will continue on into the following year.

Due to COVID-19, live court hearings are not being held. Attorneys are filing settlements electronically, and are expected to inform their clients of all of their rights. Ethical attorneys know the "bell curve" of settlements. My approach is always to get into the high end of the range. I believe I reach the middle or high end of the range in many cases. This is because I know how to assess cases within the range of the bell curve, and if we can't get there, I will recommend other options and approaches.

Some entities, such as municipalities, hospitals, school districts, and big-box stores are "self-insured", meaning the money they pay comes out of their own pockets, unlike an insurance company. When you pay from your own pocket, common sense says not to overpay for something!

Many clients are quite frustrated and disenchanted during the settlement process, and may want to just take the money that's being offered and move on. However, they'll be prevented from doing so if the judge won't approve the settlement. I have reviewed well over a thousand proposed settlements. When I see an offer that's close to the mark, I will just tell the claimant how to get the extra money without hiring an attorney if possible, and if the case is otherwise relatively straight forward.

CHAPTER 10

CAN A WORKERS' COMPENSATION SETTLEMENT IMPACT OTHER BENEFITS?

A workers' compensations settlement can affect private disability benefits, and the right to receive future medical benefits through Medi-Cal or Medicare if there is a lump sum settlement. It can also affect the receipt of Social Security disability benefits if the settlement is not properly allocated. These are complicated matters, and each case must be looked at individually by an attorney. If the settlements are not drawn up properly, it can cause unforeseen problems in the future.

How Are Settlement Amounts Calculated, And What If My Injuries Resurface Or Worsen Down The Line?

Most settlements include an amount for the dollar value of the permanent impairment/disability rating and the future medical care expenses, assuming a lump sum amount is requested. An insurance company cannot make a claimant take a lump sum settlement, and vice versa. Generally, if the worker returns to their place of employment after completing medical treatment and receiving an impairment rating, they will not recover a lump sum settlement unless the insurance company no longer insures the employer. It should also be noted that most settlements include compensation for out-of-pocket expenses, and claimants can recover mileage reimbursement to and from medical appointments. A claimant can also receive a stipulated award, which means they receive their settlement at bi-weekly intervals up to $290 per week, while retaining their right to future medical care.

WHAT ABOUT ATTORNEY FEES?

We are required to disclose that attorney fees in the amount of 9 to 15 percent are deducted from the final settlement amount. Attorneys who are certified legal specialists, such as myself, or whom otherwise have performed at a high rate of proficiency, or who carry out an extensive amount of work in obtaining an excellent and even extraordinary result may be entitled to greater than 15 percent of the total settlement amount. Each workers' compensation appeals board in California has its' ***own practices and procedures*** with regard to the handling of attorney fees. However, attorneys are not allowed to charge anything for consultations, nor are they allowed to collect any fees up front from anyone. All fee requests need to be approved by a workers' compensation administrative law judge at the time of settlement. All fees are deducted from the final settlement, regardless of whether or not there is a lump sum award.

We have heard of situations where attorneys charged an hourly fee for a consultation or otherwise charged fees for their services during the pendency of a claim; this is illegal, and will result in the attorney being severely disciplined by the State Bar of California. Many clients have offered me cash or to write me a check after a free consultation, and as much as I appreciate their generosity, I refuse such requests because I know it is illegal for these clients to have to pay me anything out of pocket for a consultation or for any services prior to receiving an approved settlement.

CHAPTER 11

SHOULD I HIRE AN ATTORNEY RIGHT AFTER AN INJURY OR WAIT FOR A DENIAL?

We generally tell our clients that we cannot do much for them until a claim form is filed. If the insurance company accepts the claim, then we have to make a judgment call as to how severe we expect the residuals to be. If the claim is being delayed or medical treatment is being denied, then it would be best to hire an attorney early on in the process, and to obtain proper medical treatment from a private doctor or a panel QME.

If a claim is denied, it is highly unlikely that the worker will be able to receive significant medical treatment through the workers' compensation system, at least in San Diego County. Under these circumstances, it would be best to obtain medical treatment through one's own individual health plan. Many physicians, however, will refuse to provide medical treatment on a work-related injury, even on a denied workers' compensation claim. This can create very murky waters for clients who are wrongfully denied medical treatment through their private health plans. We can certainly assist our clients in obtaining medical treatment, even when a claim is denied through their health plan.

Sometimes, denied claims can be settled early on in the process with lump sum settlements. Once a workers' compensation claim is settled, the worker's medical treatment should be covered by a health insurance policy, even if there are pre-existing conditions. However, it is still very common for health insurance companies to try to deny medical treatment for claimed workers' compensation benefits that are denied. This is a very complicated situation that requires a case-by-case analysis. For this reason, it is always best to consult with a practitioner early on in the process. I am very candid with potential clients about what I am and am not capable of accomplishing.

What Are The Risks Associated With Handling A Workers' Compensation Case Without An Attorney?

There are many risks associated with handling a workers' compensation case without an attorney. One of the main misconceptions is that the treating provider will conduct a thorough and accurate assessment of the full extent of the injuries, and write intelligent reports at the time of settlement. It is quite common for people to treat with doctors for a long period of time, only to eventually learn that necessary medical treatment, diagnostics, or medications are being delayed or denied because the doctor has too many patients.

Most of our clients are hardworking and seemingly honest individuals who just want to return to work and move on with their lives. However, this isn't always possible. Sometimes, clients are too trusting of their doctors, who are usually selected by the insurance companies. While I do believe that insurance claims representatives usually try to do their best, they are not in the business to give the workers the best advice that is what we do. As time goes on, workers' compensation medical benefits and the right to see particular specialists are being frittered away as doctors leave the workers' compensation system for greener pastures (i.e. higher pay and less paperwork).

Clients are often not informed of their choices in obtaining medical or chiropractic treatment through the workers' compensation system. The reality is that clients have a lot of leeway in terms of which doctor to choose as their primary care physician. For example, a client could choose an orthopedic or pain specialist, chiropractor, or even acupuncturist as a primary treating physician in the state of California. Most people do not know this, and even if they did, they wouldn't know which doctors to select from a list of nearly 300. We are often able to narrow down a list of 300 doctors to a list of about five or 10 doctors. Once we accomplish that, we can obtain immediate medical appointments for our clients. We have had some clients who are treating with a highly skilled orthopedic spine surgeon for a non-surgical shoulder or knee injury. I cannot explain why this would happen, and suffice it to say that a spine surgeon may understand general orthopedics as it relates to the affected knee or shoulder, that body part is not their particular specialty. There are auto mechanics who can work on one particular part of a transmission, but know nothing about tires or mufflers; the same holds true for the human body.

The important thing to note is that the sooner someone sees the appropriate medical provider, the sooner that person can receive proper treatment, and hopefully get better. We recognize the frustration our clients have when they call us, but the truth of the matter is that most clients wish they'd called us sooner. In the same way that it is not a doctor's job to chastise their patients for not quitting smoking, not losing weight, or not reducing their alcohol consumption, it is not my job to chastise the general public for not understanding the rules of the workers' compensation claims system. My job is to help clients efficiently and quickly navigate the workers' compensation system.

Like a chef who knows recipes like the back of their hand or a mechanic who doesn't have to consult the auto manual in order to fix a transmission, I am simply a legal technician who understands the law and knows how to identify the proper solution for a particular problem.

CHAPTER 12

WHAT SETS YOU AND YOUR LAW FIRM APART?

Prior to becoming an attorney in 1989, I had some experience as a law clerk in handling personal injury, criminal and divorce cases. I also worked as a private investigator for San Diego County in the mid 1980's. Early on in my legal practice, I was contacted by a number of doctors who wanted me to help their patients in workers' compensation cases. It became abundantly clear to me that many workers'

compensation attorneys have a volume-based practice and handle every case more or less in the same way.

I have always tried to provide a higher level of integrity and personalized service to my clients. I also realize some clients have unrealistic expectations about what attorneys can and cannot accomplish, and that this career is similar to being a social worker at times. In the early days, I set out to market my referral sources within the local San Diego legal community. I always felt it was necessary to respond to phone calls in a timely fashion, and I surrounded myself with skilled, well-trained support staff. As a result, almost 33 years later, my practice is almost exclusively referral-based.

I feel very passionate about my role in obtaining both proper medical treatment and getting the maximum amount of medical benefits available under the law. I recognize that most people would not be in my office unless they really needed to be. There seems to be a perception that most workers' compensation clients don't want to get better and don't want to return to work, but I have not found that to be the case.

When Arnold Schwarzenegger became the governor of California in 2004, he overhauled the workers' compensation system such that a person's ultimate monetary settlement would be based on an impairment, when before this it was based on an individual's work restrictions or disability. The important distinction to be made is this: an impairment is a dysfunction in a body part, whereas a disability is an inability or reduced ability to work in the open labor market. Some people who may have what seems to be a minor neck injury tell me that they can never work again.

On the other hand, there are people who undergo serious neck surgeries, but who are able to return to their jobs because they get paid well and have an employer who can accommodate their restrictions. Despite having a high level of impairment from a percentage standpoint, such an individual may continue to do their job every day. Consider, for example, a professional football player who undergoes a back surgery. Under contract to perform, they may return to work and play full-contact football every day. This football player would have the same level of impairment as a construction worker or an office worker who underwent the same type of surgery. In other words, the workers' compensation system does not reward a person for not working or for having a higher level of disability, nor does it penalize a person who is able to return to work. The only difference would be the type of settlement they receive. Remember, if a person returns to the job where they got hurt, they probably won't be eligible for a lump sum settlement. Why would an employer want to compensate someone for future medical expenses when the person can still file a whole new claim if there is a 1% aggravation of a prior physical injury?

As another example, consider a construction worker who cuts off part of his index finger; this type of injury would probably result in a three to eight percent impairment rating. If that construction worker were to return to the same work site and continue to do their job, and if that company were to eventually close, then the insurance company might tell them that they are eligible for a settlement. If that worker were to call me and ask what amount I could help them obtain, I might say $20,000 to $25,000. In all likelihood, that worker would be very pleased, having previously assumed that they weren't eligible for a settlement to begin with.

Now consider a different scenario; one in which an orthopedic surgeon, who as a result of not paying attention to what he was doing, cut off the second digit of his index finger. It is highly likely that as a physician, he would never be able to perform surgery again. Under these circumstances, the surgeon's anatomical rating would be the same as the construction worker's anatomical rating, despite the fact that the construction worker was able to return to work and the surgeon was not.

The point that I make is this: I aim to put each case in its best light given the particular facts. There are many limitations in the workers' compensation system; settlements have decreased as medical costs have decreased, and insurance companies no longer pay large amounts of money for future medical expenses.

In all reality, I think the best that I can do is provide an accurate assessment of each claim to each client based on the particular facts of their case. When someone consults with me, I avoid discussion of the amount of money I can recover at the end of the case. Recently, a potential client said that two other attorneys said they could get $75,000 for the claim, and I told the potential client that there is no way for an attorney to know that. This is because there are simply too many variables involved, and the settlement amount would depend upon the residual effects of the injuries and future medical costs.

In many cases, I believe it's important for people to obtain opinions from different attorneys before hiring one. Many of my clients come to me with excellent references from their family members or other attorneys, so they know they are going to hire me prior to even speaking to me. While that's quite flattering, I frequently advise clients to talk to other reputable attorneys—especially if they are on the fence about hiring me. I want them to feel free to ask a number of questions to a number of attorneys without fear of reprisal. If someone asks me a question and I cannot answer it, I'll be honest and tell them that I do not have the answer; I would never just make up an answer in an attempt to appease a potential or current client.

It is also important for people to confirm that the attorney they hire is responsible and has an unblemished record with the State Bar of California, which can be determined by visiting www.calbar.ca.gov. People should know whether an attorney carries malpractice or liability insurance in case things go south (my firm has malpractice insurance, but some do not). It is important for people to know that if they are unhappy with their attorney, they have the right to change attorneys at any time and for any reason.

Some clients tell me they want to fire their lawyers. I frequently recommend that they try to resolve their disputes with the attorney first. Some attorneys are accused of not returning phone calls or emails, and/or of not personally communicating with clients. While it is important for people to understand that attorneys are very busy people who are usually handling many cases at once, I believe it's also important for them to feel that they can speak with the attorney when necessary. Most of my clients' inquiries can easily be handled by the support staff, but I make it very clear that the buck stops with me. This means that if a client needs to speak with me or is not satisfied with the responses from my staff, they can schedule a telephone appointment or Zoom meeting, or can communicate with me directly via email so that I can answer their questions and concerns sufficiently.

That being said, there are clients who sometimes forget that we are not available 24/7, 365 days a year, evenings, weekends, or holidays. As a result, some clients develop the tendency to call with any particular question at any given time, multiple times per week. This is kind of a red flag situation; if a client wants to maintain a harmonious relationship with their legal counsel, they should try to ask multiple questions at the same time, rather than call each day with a different question. I understand that clients have a lot of concerns and anxiety over the entire workers' compensation process. For this reason, I make sure to cover all of the pertinent information in my initial letters. However, I also want clients to know that they should feel free to call me if questions arise, especially those with regard to the often-confusing forms and letters sent by insurance companies.

It is my hope that clients remember that attorneys and support staff are human beings too; we bleed, we have family emergencies, we get sick, we go on vacation, and we make mistakes. I have always said that the reason pencils have erasers is because people make mistakes. With that said, I realize that it's my name on the office door, which means if something is not handled to the satisfaction of the client, I am not going to blame my support staff or anyone else for the creation of the problem; I will accept responsibility at all times and do everything I can to correct the issue.

A common complaint from clients is that their disability checks are delayed or don't arrive at all, or that they have not been properly reimbursed for mileage. Insurance companies generally have 60 days to respond to mileage reimbursement requests; if they pay it on the 65th day, it's usually not a big deal. Clients are supposed to receive their biweekly temporary disability checks on a specific day of the week, every two weeks (without delay). Due to no fault of the attorney or insurance company, certain events can cause a delay of two or three days (e.g. holidays, a glitch in the mail system, human error). For this reason, it's advisable that clients not write checks before confirming that they have money in their account, and it is not advisable that clients yell at or use bad language when speaking with the attorney or support staff.

After over 30 years in practice, I believe our reputation speaks for itself because we receive referrals from some very fine attorneys and people whom I've known for many years. No one is perfect, but we do understand how important it is to be reasonable and maintain composure during difficult times. When a client shows that they are incapable of doing the same, such as by yelling, cursing, or calling every single day, then we (and most other attorneys) likely won't choose to continue representing that client. Fortunately, this is rarely the case at our firm because we vet our cases and clients somewhat carefully in order to avoid difficult personalities. At the same time, we do recognize that many clients are injured and extremely anxious about their situation, and we try our best to be sympathetic to that. As an attorney, my goal is to handle each and every case in the most efficient and effective manner possible.

INDEX

U

W

Notes

Made in the USA
Monee, IL
05 November 2026

67387966R00059